Reconnaissance

Reconnaissance

Amy Nawrocki

HOMEBOUND
PUBLICATIONS
Independent Publisher of Contemplative Titles
STONINGTON, CONNECTICUT

PUBLISHED BY HOMEBOUND PUBLICATIONS

For bulk ordering information or permissions write:
Homebound Publications, PO Box 1442
Pawcatuck, Connecticut 06379 United States of America
Visit us at: www.homeboundpublications.com
Visit the author at: www.amynawrocki.org

FIRST EDITION
ISBN: 978-1-938846-69-4 (pbk)

BOOK DESIGN
Front Cover Image: © *Wheatstacks, Snow Effect, Morning,* 1891,
by Claude Monet
Digital image courtesy of the Getty's Open Content Program.
Cover and Interior Design: Leslie M. Browning

Library of Congress Cataloging-in-Publication Data

Nawrocki, Amy.
[Poems. Selections]
Reconnaissance : poems / by Amy Nawrocki. -- First edition.
pages cm
ISBN 978-1-938846-69-4 (pbk.)
I. Title.
PS3614.A934A6 2015
811'.6--dc23

2014048554

10 9 8 7 6 5 4 3 2 1

Homebound Publications holds a fervor for environmental conservation. Atop donating a percentage of our annual income to an ecological charity, we are ever-mindful of our "carbon footprint". Our books are printed on paper with chain of custody certification from the Forest Stewardship Council, Sustainable Forestry Initiative, and the Programme for the Endorsement of Forest Certification. This ensures that, in every step of the process, from the tree to the reader's hands, the paper our books are printed on has come from sustainably managed forests.

Also by Amy Nawrocki

Poetry Collections

Potato Eaters
Nomad's End
Lune de Miel
Four Blue Eggs

Coauthored with Eric D. Lehman

A History of Connecticut Wine
A History of Connecticut Food
Literary Connecticut

Acknowledgements

Grateful acknowledgement is given to the editors of the following journals and publications in which poems from this collection previously appeared or were honored, sometimes in earlier forms:

Connecticut Poetry Society: "Noah and the Cave"
Connecticut River Review: "Love the Trumpet"
Garbanzo Literary Journal: "Making Love to Lord Byron on the Morning of My Thirty-seventh Birthday"
The Loft Poetry Anthology, *Lay Bare the Canvas: New England Poets on Art*: "Smoke of Ambergris"
New Millennium Writings: "How to Visit your Alma Mater"
White Leaf Review, and the *White Leaf Anthology*: "Some Things Are Best Left"

Special appreciation is given to Finishing Line Press, publishers of the chapbook *Lune de Miel*, where the following poems were first collected: "Cimetìere du Père Lachaise," "Translating the Shrew," "When Will You Marry," "Reading Anaïs Nin," and "After Inspecting Brassaï's Graffiti"

William Burroughs' quote comes from his lecture "First Thought Best Thought." The quote "Open thy mouth and eat what I give thee" is from Ezekiel 2:8. The quote "There was an occupation" comes from *Tender Buttons* by Gertrude Stein.

Contents

The writer does not own words any more than the painter owns colors. So let's dispense with this originality fetish.

—William S. Burroughs

Guided Tour

Memorize a few loose-leaf pages,
note important dates with precision. Mention
the children by name and explain the heritage
of the highboy in the parlor—cherry, late 18th century,
brass fixtures, replacements, not original.
Demonstrate the peculiar habits
of instruments placed with emphasis
around the house: pretend to fill
the tin-top foot warmers with hot coals,
mimic the dipping of candle wicks
in and out of their molds, smile coyly
as you tighten the rope mattress
with the antique bed key the way
someone would have two hundred years ago.

At times you recognize a twinge
of inaccuracy in the script, something
tinkering toward futility escaping
in your voice. And for a few minutes
as you watch visitors wave back
on their way to the car you wonder
if a pleasant tone and a few lucky cobwebs
are enough to recapture the history of a farmhouse
or of inhabitants who never seem to leave
enough behind. The past seems repetitive

until a blind man who need help placing
his feet up stone steps, bends into a prayer pose
and touches the floor's pine planks
with both hands. Through the kitchen
and side bedrooms, past looms and the old

rocking horse, he feels his way and measures
distances with small steps. He knows
without being told that we've returned
to the front entrance, "where we started."

Miss Roberts and *The Works of Percy Bysshe Shelley*

The MacMillan Company published the edition
in 1908, a textured green cover and gold trim
holding together with little wear, white edges
beginning to peek from rounding corners.
A century later, the collection found its way
to the woody shelves of a barn. Bound
with shadowy poems cast on type-set pages
the book's life crafts a correspondence of its own.

Jettisoned into the folio's deckled leafs,
a calling card left decades ago slips out
and falls on a table. The name printed neatly
in small elegant script: *Miss Roberts;* tails
curl inquisitively from beneath M and R.
With a black fountain pen, she crossed out
formality and scribbled her first name: *Bess.*
On the reverse, the message that would escort
Shelley's poems to an upstairs room where
a man had decided he no longer craved her smile:
lots and lots of love, she wrote in haste, crossing
t's so that the ink missed their intersection, *and*
congratulations. His wife would have the child.

Perhaps writing her name would touch him
somehow, perhaps the printer's toil, setting
letter after letter onto the press, rolling thin ink,
would tell him of dedication, perhaps
Percy's love for Mary would cross the t's
that she could not. A century of unfinished
correspondence never read: the quarto pages
remained uncut by any reader's knife.

"Open thy mouth and eat what I give thee"

—after Chagall's stained glass, Union Church,
Pocantico Hills, NY

Where syllogisms fail, there is faith,
and for some that may be enough. But
for others, more than devotion
heats silica and cobalt oxide, pours it
around lead threads, and mounts it
between brick and the exposed,
colorless fallout of photons. If we believe

in god and that he created sentient men,
and that these men speak with forged instruments
and sing with unnatural beauty, then it is god
who is speaking, and who among us could not
stomach that contract? If god wills Ezekiel
to swallow the sacred scroll, then he allows
Marc Chagall to escape the burden
of his birth and war's pointed fingers,
stir nightmares on opera ceilings and float
goats in the red haze of paint while
the children of Israel march toward iron fires
and fall into graves dug by god himself.

Made in our father's image, we are people
of strange speech and hard language;
hallelujahs cracked and splayed
like wolf carcasses on crosses: curses
rumble beneath our hearing. We eat our own
words and fill bowels with confessions, make
graven images with blind heliotropic devotion.
Even prophets bathed in leaden light
cannot break our tongues or shield us
from derelict and capricious fates.

Noah and the Cave

The newborn sea-cave
traps a puddle, and a sheen
filters from a moon
that has settled not too far,
a blossom caught on the end

of a long string,
bulbous and wanting. He wakes,
shaken by the wind;
the honey-gold wine has waned,
but the stomach sours still,

his mind wedged
between thoughts of the platypus,
the ruby-black water,
and his own bare skin. Wishing
for the purge, for a spindle

of wool, for the salt
in his veins to sugar over—
for a rainbow—
he closes his eyes again
and drops his face in the puddle

and dreams. The night finds
its close; his lungs fill as tides
pull the ocean
to and from the shore, a band
of waves severs the breath.

When his sons find him
and clothe his naked skin,

the acquiescence
of light to darkness
echoes through the cave—the task

of rescue too broad
for his bones to maintain.
Every animal
saved, the world populated,
yet only a dove can sustain

this zoology
for long. In the lean puddle
he found painless defeat
in the shortage of water,
the cradle of human drought.

The Thief

I apprenticed well. For a sixth grade project,
Mrs. Montecalvo taught me the worth
of a good forgery when she assigned
the footnoted history of a painter
and encouraged an attempt at imitation.
Seeing Monet's *Westminster Bridge* reprinted
in *Reader's Digest,* I modeled my own
with schoolgirl brushes and an aptitude
for blending. I typed his biography
on a blue Remington, stenciled a title page,
punched symmetrical holes and glued
the masterpiece into a pocketed folder.
I never got the stink of acrylic off my fingers.

Audacity and small victories: these
are gateways for any scavenger.
Once one is secure in the false flat
of a sloped horizon, transformations
are easy: an open book, so to speak.

I pocketed the *Collected Poems*
of ee cummings wholesale, tore
the bar code from the last page
and slipped its frayed spine between
loose-leaf sheets of unlined
but perforated notebooks. Long after,
the card catalog entry went away too.

Like other trophies, I just stored it,
held it in a box of pressed flowers
and half memorized poems, among

generous piles of pens and paint brushes,
newspaper clippings and dirty love letters
scribbled on the backs of postcards.

For these corruptions I've paid only
in callouses and broken pencil tips.
Despite my best calligraphy,
slippery pens have crossed out
entire lines carefully typeset in Linotype
or Century Schoolbook, my marks bleeding
through pages now unreadable.

In the gray area between homage
and sacrilege, I thieve too much:
red wheelbarrows pile full of leaves and dirt
and burnable logs pressed into the pulp
of scrap paper or woven into stretchable
canvases. Little I see in nature
that is my own. I stole van Gogh's sadness
and painted it on my shoulder.
Like Olympia, I learned how to stare.

Next time, let me mimic the syntax of bridges
and throw sand over wet, stolen ink.
Let me trust in surveillance. Once the thief
learns to discern *original* from *run of the mill*
everything is a first edition; everything
is one of a kind.

Smoke of Ambergris

—after *Fumée d'Ambre Gris*, by John Singer Sargent

There are no clocks in the marketplace
but timekeepers eavesdrop everywhere
and beckon like thieves into robed corners
of gypsum alabaster. The incense lasts until
its burden is released, until the urn's flame
is beheaded or the sweet cardamom echoes
filter from the minarets too far to visit. Unseen

tarnish signals the souring of metal pounded
in rhythmic intervals and of a heart hidden
under pale yellow crepe that failed to beat just once
when the dagger struck and the blood
which she could not cleanse from closed eyes
drained out of him onto a different rug,
one with cerulean threads, one woven by herders,
caravanned by camels and lastly burned by finality

because there was nothing else to do to stop
those immeasurable, mysterious wakings
from repeating with each night's darkness.

To mute the sun's piquant tongue, one
remedy remains untapped: the sea and its blunder
of debris, the bile of a lost whale, the mute
gray smoke of sorcery's deep inhalation,
and the elegant crucible of a held breath.

After Making Love to Lord Byron on the Morning of My Thirty-seventh Birthday

He left me once the broken blue
of dawn came through the window,
at the instant when night and day
drew apart. But like all heroes
with sable hair and burnt eyes, darkness
eclipses the rose of soft lips, and a kiss,

well, no woman can expect such a goodbye,
not even on her birthday. The kitchen hisses
with the hot hiccup of animal flesh
burning on the stove. I finish coffee
and fill my belly with warm toast, wait to end
the day with wine. There are no candles today.

As I write another year, the brooding exile
in my bed slumbers in a claret robe forever
in the fever of thirty six. We'll go no more
a-roving, except to the phantom hearth where he
will wait for me. The ink of my pen
burns into the woven fibers of a sheet.

Cimetìere du Père Lachaise

As I bend down to add my lips
to the dead kisses on Oscar Wilde's tombstone,
I can't help but laugh
and wish there were a more punishing word
for *irony* than the one we have.
When cemeteries bloom, death seems
less distant, and I guess that is the point.
Père Lachaise is a city—with maps,
street signs, and pedestrians, houses full
of memories, full of fame, history, and life.
Music and art settle here: Chopin hums
Prelude number 6, Pissarro washes paintbrushes
with tears. In search of names, the living carry
freshly cut flowers, and green, perpetual moss
swaddles dead tombs. I hold onto my husband,
in this blooming winter, the first day of a new year,
and we roam without sadness through stone,
twist to an outer road where names disappear

and skeletons sculpted with the fire of remembrance
bear the stark metonymy of place:
Dachau, Buchenwald, Ravensbrück.
Only the screeching purple birds smell
the paradox: lilies and roses can never unpollute
the stench of burning yellow stars.

Japanese Lady on a Lacquered Stand

She is nameless, like the far away snow caps of *Fuji-san* before winds tainted our notions of what we tell. For as long as memory has suffered the house, the Japanese doll remained a living room fixture, boarded in a glass display box, a relic of a story no one knew. All those years, only the smallest granule of dust reached her. We never knew how she came to be.

most stories are lost
in ebony hair, drawn tightly
by the red cords of a straw hat

Maybe Uncle Herb, the carpet trader, smuggled her in a handle-less trunk. Mother's college trip to California seems a more likely culprit; the Kodak slides projected on the blank wall one Christmas may have confirmed her interest in Japanese collectables. Most probable is this: Father's exaggerated episodes of navy adventures noosed their way into the tight knot of her hair. He liked to weave yarns about days spent in the Orient, though we know he never served in Japan, never saw the Silk Road or cherry blossoms dancing in front of Shinto shrines. He saw only Moroccan deserts and German Alps. Japan, like ebony nuggets of truth, existed only in his mind.

these unknowable
silences strum in the folds
of lost kimonos

In her miniature world, she poses with patient shyness, stuffed with dried stalks and costumed in amber silk dress and beige *obi* sash. Black cranes dance in the folds of her dress which falls to ankles clad in straw *zori* sandals. With powdered face and brushed black eyes, she will never part her painted lips. Small crepe fingers, like long grains of rice, perpetually pluck three strings of a *shamisen*.

scrapbook mutations
silent movies, chronicles
buried with the dead

We imagine she came to us from the deep, where silence is spoken and the bamboo boats of nostalgia struggle across a hopeless ocean. Giant waves pummeled her lonely vessel, but something akin to music escaped from her tight lips, keeping away sea monsters with their giant teeth. Something akin to moonlight kept the straw dry and the thread strings of her lyre unbroken.

(Not) A Thousand Words

Somewhere in the vicinity of 1943, a fisherman
throws his net over a sea that has no color.
A camera snaps; the moment deserves

its preservation. The album's black pages and perfectly
posed triangle edges hold remainders of few years.
Somewhere in the vicinity of 1943, a navy recruit

departs Rhode Island for Jacksonville, the only destinations
noted in black ink on white bordered photographs.
The camera snaps and those moments desert

time, passed over by a faraway, unnamed island's coconuts
and grass skirts shielding the volcano future of midshipmen.
Somewhere in the vicinity of World War Two

Stanley joined Poseidon's band of sea brawlers, all of whom
prefer tropical girls to destroyers and sea sickness.
A camera snaps, the moment demolished

in barracks. Seventy years later a fisherman tosses
a net over a sea that has no color—the fisherman's chronicler
lost somewhere in the vicinity of a photo album.
A camera snaps only the undeserving moments.

Preparing the Bonsai

It pretends
toward age.
The master's hands sculpt
the tree into a dwarf
masquerading
as an ancient who has weathered
nature's acute spells
and survived.

The pine
endures the discipline
of thin wire
and pruning shears
and lives
as art.

I cannot help
but think of bound feet,
silk wound tightly
around small toes, roots
cramped and hobbled
without ground to spread.

The bonsai
who waits as a seed
in a cloak of soggy peat
is a mask, a
pretender
posing as philosopher
its clay bowl abode
already dwarfing the bud.

Long Shot

A good snapshot stops a moment from running away.
—Eudora Welty

The dilemma is not
about choosing between
architecture or faces,
panorama or close-up,
indirect light or flash

but between
the print's future frame
and the quiet immobility
of reflection—of just sitting
and being, not worrying
about whether any of this
will be preserved digitally
and remembered in twelve
or thirteen years. Chances are,

tomorrow I will struggle
with recreating the bird
swaggering near my feet. Maybe
in some somnambulant day dream,
I'll re-see these tiny
daisy-like weeds and hear
the passersby crunch gravel
under lazy sneakers. I might
be able to gather pieces
of foil and flattened cigarettes
instead of fading poppies
or the leaves of a tree
I cannot name
blowing in a breeze.

It would be easier
if I didn't love
every single pigeon—this one
with his spooky eyes and orange beak,
a single brushstroke
of white and teal beneath his neck—
and if the fence's shadow
wasn't so dappled and transient,
if acorns would stop falling
mid-distance between dawn
and dusk, long enough
to preserve their posts
in my mind, if forgoing

the shot and closing my eyes
would be enough to argue against
some future self
who will be too old or sad
or something worse
to remember this.

The Charity Houses of Cape Cod

This is what Thoreau
called those rickety
and shingled bungalows

that braced the wind-swept
dune sands with the kind
of poise given to

the most humble
of structures, when
wooden planks know

they are no match
for the tyranny
and heartlessness

of sea storms. When
he walked along
the Cape Cod shoreline,

Thoreau's mapmaker feet
followed the path
his mind sought between

the Nauset Plains
and Highland Light,
the urge to become

a little more salted
seeping into his skin.
In these small shacks

he found company,
even when no other souls
were about—comfort

from a lonely stretch
of steady, barren beach.
Shelter, whatever

form it takes—whether
the lucky shade
of the high cumulus,

or the calm, temporary
sedation of low tide,
or even a sloped roof

suspended with the architecture
of nails and grooved logs
over a dry, simple place—shelter

gives respite of the sort
that clams know
pausing in the sand

before the gulls
with their appetite and spite
return to feed.

The man sitting next to me is reading *The Idiot,*

and everyone seems to be engaged in conversation:
two regulars *parler* in quick sentences, the thin one appoints
the red-cravated waiter. Two blonde women suggest

with their hands that they do not care about the silent man
sitting by himself, biting the side of his mouth, staring at bicycles.
Everyone seems to be engaged in conversation

stuck in the lobes of their ears. A pair of shaded specs
speak without words to numbers on a cell phone.
The red-cravated waiter sulks; two blonde women suggest

replacing the used lemon that sits crosswise and upright
against the side of the glass. The glass drips, melted like
conversations everyone seems to be engaged in

with lips thrust together in puckered slopes toward
unused air, not pronouncing all those extra letters
the red-cravated waiter holds in his pocket suggesting

the answer to questions asked by the cigarette dangling
from an unlit mouth mirrored in the silent man's cup.
Everyone seems to be engaged in conversation with *eau de vie*
as the red-cravated waiter and two blonde women suggest.

The Fifth Window

The painting above the wicker chair
interprets a garden. Outside, behind
the outline of a window, fence posts
aslant to the house mimic a trellis.

These are two windows. One
to the exterior world of green
and overgrown weeds,
some flowering and some not.

The other frames an interior—a place
imagined and permanent.
And these two views do not argue
but shine equally—two dimensions

of an unflat world. The hum
of the fan echoing through both
or neither, depending
on who's listening, depending

on who's watching.
In front of the sink, the third
window is a mirror, and into it
I see my paned windows, curtains,

and green. It's a good view—
but the end of blackberries,
knobbed and white, unripe or ripening—
are not visible from the mirror.

Maybe the wall's window—the painting—
misses them too. They're too small,
too prickly, too distant. I tilt
my head over the white pane and see

a daylily open and point toward
another window—the sea—not too
far off. The painting has neither
the daylily nor the sea, and I am sorry

for its rooted gaze, though
I understand the comfort held
in one seductive yet inert frame.
But tomorrow's review will create

a new garden, ripe berries, perhaps
lavender or gold, and another eye
who sees something entirely different
something perfectly un-true.

What Jodie Taught Me about Tattoos

—for Jodie Lane

She could not be buried,
her father told her,
with ink scalpelled into skin,
defacement of the body
prohibited by Jewish law.
With spider legs painted
around skull's demon visage,
she wore hers without apology
under stringy tank tops
and the ripped sarcasm
of baggy sweats around
a petite frame. She confided
obsessions over cigarettes
blurred into the falling leaves
of freshman year laughing,
never telling stories
of spiders or skulls, not minding
the sunflower I chose
for my own mark. We wanted
to ink into the eternal, forge
the intransient specter
of adulthood with scars
of our own making.

The last time I saw her
we sat for coffee between
darkened booths at the local
diner. A postcard sent
from Texas came a few years
later and then abbreviated

obituary lines stapled
between the alumni magazine,
electrocution, freak
accident walking dogs,
voltage engraving her body
with ungrounded shrieks
through a Manhattan sidewalk.

East 11th street is pocketed
with sewer drains and manholes,
and a street sign marks
the site where she fell.
I stare up into the permanence
of the story, one I kept hidden
in the flower on my shoulder,
the rumor of loss now etched
in visible lettering across
an overcast sky, persisting
beyond a combustible
and porous layer of skin.

Translating the Shrew

We cannot hear the passing of centuries
so easily; we think we can drum into
a clatter heard four hundred years ago
by opening pages, staging the play
with modern twists, mirrors and placard props,
avant-garde lighting, *en français*, no less.
Waiting for the curtain to rise, we listen
to *l'histore de la Comédie-Française,*
tap the glass around Molière's frayed chair,
imagine quills slipped in ink scraping across
yellowed parchment, eavesdrop with Anglo ears
to the taming of Katherine of Padua;
but there's no adequate way to hear
Kate's voice, unless we shatter the mirrors
and listen as the shards tell us who we really are.

Distilling Sol Lewitt

Obliterate, says the line,
curve the horizon, resist
tremors of an inexact hand,
tap into the statuesque control
of an oblique axis, linger
in the infinite advance; find proof
of existence between the abscissa
and the ordinate, between Euclid
and Descartes, between an arrow
and its trajectory.

The Rothko Conundrum

—the Phillips Collection

1.
binary hypothesis
recognizable. a door
two mirrors. eight cauldrons
a house with its roof
green wishing away a marooned horizon

a blood puddle laying
on the upturned walkway
the puddle pretending a dance
the mirror between

2.
an upside-down paragraph
hapless bronze fire
waking the vertical

bottle glass wishing away a citrus horizon
unfinished books. the last pieces
of paper left on the floor
perpendicular mischief

3.
lost fish music. horizontal longing. orange and red on red
wishing away a missing horizon
lost in watertight cathedral windows
burdenless aches. plurality

the singular capture of loss
knowing or not knowing the ending

4.

the house next door
a second window, serenity
ochre hallelujahs caught
on the windowsill
kneeling inside emptiness
sore fences. twice pink horizon

where seraphs go
why envelopes open
quadrilaterally quiet
five times red

Poem for Salvador Dali upon the Occasion of Winning His Lithograph at an Auction

I dreamt last night of a moustache,
the corpulent pockets of my brain abuzz
with blue women. In the penciled curves
of your signature, I hide from the gadget
now unframed from the screen,
a crippled apparatus with wanting
legs staggering toward me.
You are not in my dreams
as a demon, but a caned intruder
with fleshless hand, stroking
my insides, the tang of rot
on your fingers. I am just a pauper,
collecting wall space and filling it
with veins and artifice, headless torsos,
the far-away bubble of hills. I clock
memory as persistently
as your hand does reaching out
from the blue of a flightless wall.

Love the Trumpet

The doctors invited me to be still.
Then the X-ray revealed
one of van Gogh's sunflowers
dying inside me, just beneath my ribs.
Not enough sun, they said,
prescribed antibiotics and suggested
lemon juice to ease the pain.
That was when I started
dreaming in stereo
and playing the trumpet
inside a building with glass walls.

Mountains of light get trapped,
and sometimes I make the glass move
with a thick and wasted rhythm,
my fingers burning like tin haystacks
every time I play high C. I try so hard
but I end up with photosynthesis
on my hands and still that sunflower
huddles wilting beneath my bones.
Every morning I wake up
spitting pollen onto the bed sheets.

For eight years now I've slept
without a legitimate pillow. My trumpet
has suffered and I dream about Arles.
I'm so out of practice; when I play
somehow I mutilate all the prisms:
the rainbows misplace blue
and green has disappeared completely.
I have to wear sunglasses and steel-toed shoes

because that sunlight keeps biting me
like a rabid dog. The doctors
find a million ways to tell me
a cure is a million years away.
But I just can't keep playing the trumpet
when I'm foaming at the mouth.

Desperation

—after Theodore Roethke

I have known the inexact squalor of diagnoses
scrawled onto script pads, hidden in desolate folders
sold to drug reps and financed by urine and blood;
paper robes opening in the back, pillowless
vinyl tables and the barbed slurp of syringes,
negotiating between the silent vertebrae
of a prostrate spine, the silhouette of bones
mapped by magnets and ghostly as snow.

I have seen corrupt fluids sucked into vials,
held my breath in a cave as the echoes resonated
like a tomb song, waited in barren rooms alone
with pamphlets folded by machines and stapled
at perfect creases, bearing the polysyllabic
names of tablets and the nauseous promise of loss.

Ode to My Brain

How you itch inside my skull, quaking
with the synaptic pulse of a curling rock
or a snow shower predictably inching across
a brightly colored map, gray and white and pink.
Stop itching, you silly brain.

I see your kind in the pages of a magazine.
You're particularly glossy now, popular,
invested, researched. In the centerfold happiness,
I don't spot any scars; they must be hiding, careful
not to outshine the wires and amoeba tendrils

of lit nerves and cameras mounted on needle tips.
There is no place for your slowness or solipsism.
But I love your kindergarten messiness,
your balance exercises and key finding techniques.
No one can tell. One day, when the wheels come

and you forget all vanity, I'll remember how
even when ghostly white showed itself on the scans
you never took the time to feel sorry for yourself
or let those smudges blur your sympathy
for pollywogs and miniature spoons.

You've kept the palace swept clean of
state capitals, Egyptian pharaohs, *Gravity's
Rainbow*, and the things that happened
in 1992, leaving room for a million snapshots
of my husband's face, the yesterdays I've spent

within his gaze, echo of his voice looping
like a red scarf around you. I will scratch,
take on the punishment of needles, suffer
the cane if you will shine memory's projector
towards his eyes, his lips, his smile.

Justifying the Ways of Animals to God

Having little or no knowledge
about the fall of man,
the boy approaches the ringneck
with the zeal of a crusader
without pausing, as there is
nothing eternal to consider.

The confession had been shed already:
flaky, transparent skin hidden
beneath a rug in the unheated summer room—
the yellow necklace collaring
a brand-new black form.

The saga unfolds quietly
unaided by the dramatic pauses
of scripture nor capped off
with sermons on forgiveness.
The bite is swift, but not final:
there must be suffering.

Rebellion, pride, seduction—
these do not enter the minds of snakes
and a cat cannot tell a fallen angel
from a demon dancing
in the living room's haloed light.

Organics

—Glencoe

The coal fire at King's House
heats a steadfast room
but the smoke does not bother
a ceiling spider. Sprigs
of thistle and heather pose
in a table vase not far
from the fireplace
where nuggets of compressed wood
burn into a charred orange glow.
Buachaille Etive Mor—
the Great Herdsman—watches sheep
in front of the picture window.

Coal holds on to its centuries
unringed by what we call age.
Old as it is, the same stock
of energy warmed this room when
the Duke of Cumberland foraged
for Jacobites a century before
William Wordsworth and his sister
Dorothy slept where we sleep
and stepped where we walk. What else
has this coal witnessed? We burn fossils
to dissolve the past, stave off its blackness.

Here in the highlands, the damp
brings much renewal, much that is green,
just hatched, recently blossomed,
committed to existence for only
a heartbeat or incomplete moment.

But elsewhere across the glens
beneath the bed skirt of grass
and beyond depths that not even
a bog's seeping water can touch,
the earth remembers the unendurable,
compresses it into darkness in order
to bandage its ancient bloodlines.

When Will You Marry?

—after Gauguin's painting

They pose listening to the earth breathe instructions
from the distant rumor of mountains
who say *find happiness in a coconut.*

The orange warmth of Tahitian soil
weds land to water, fig trees
to meadow grass, the deep underbrush
to the fragrant odor of tangerine.

With skin brown as tree bark,
two sisters will grant nothing yet,
their lip like mangoes closed in mystery.

Sitting poised, an older gaze harbors suspicion
as she hides secrets in the high collar of coral dress.
Pointing ahead, marriage already stings her face.

The younger, a narcissus in her ear, slides
the top of her dress slightly off the shoulder,
icy blue splashed across bare brown skin.
Her skirt marries the hues of earth: orange to vermilion.

They are not wondering about each other now
not their suitors back from the banana harvest
nor the spill left over from the watering can

but asking—when will *you* marry,
girl of the far-away world,
who has no dark Tahitian skin to drink the sunshine
no loose-fitting clothing,
no coconuts, nor orange
to kindle the warmth of the world.

If Wishes Were Horses

The centaur looks out on the terrain
of treacherous hillocks and eroded mesas
and feels at once both lucky and complete.
Man, horse, a compromise of stolen bones—
everybody wins. Now he is capable
of trampling a thief or roping a stallion until
its neck topples and the weight of its body crashing
shakes nearby cactus needles. They all fall
to the ground. Now he can pick the barbs
one by one out of a shiny sable coat,
stampede to the earth's other side where newly
plowed orchards await with easily graspable fruit.

The aim of creation, even for unimaginative gods,
is to make the better self, to synthesize the most
perfect parts of what already exists: a block
from stone, a sprig of sumac, axle and wheel,
torso and limb, a few useless toes. The power
to extract wind, to make the catapult
newer, better, more precise—the less broken
prototype for tomorrow's wide forgetfulness.

Seeing the completion, the centaur's architect
discovers the inheritable lament for things
once certain: the mane now gone, transferred
to the an untamed scalp, a neck no longer sloped
and sure, a long face whose eyes and deep nostrils
are not improved with round skull and curved ears.

On four legs, no pirouettes spin on singular toes.
The foot now quadrupled cannot remember

how to place itself down and find balance at the end
of the twirl. There is no embrace of facing bodies
or remembering the open fence between pasture
and farm where two walked on dissimilar legs
toward the once wild grasses which tempted
both with the promise of work.

Aurelie's Jazz Collection

The tactile days of vinyl are gone, no longer
do wide black disks fit tightly into paper jackets,
nor do diamonds stroke tight grooves
and feel the coiled Braille story of the record.
Satchmo remains, his face framed
in black and white and eyeing the shelves
of CDs with a shrug of laughter, yearning
for turntable revolutions. What little we knew
of our absent French host becomes more tangible
as soon as we explore the cramped apartment—
our honeymoon home. Long crepe curtains drape
the small loft in crimson light, dull lamps hold
their dimness with the acuteness of listeners
in a Jazz club. The collection captures us:
pucker and blow of dizzying lips to trumpet
after trumpet, wet saxophone reeds; a slow
trombone slithers and hands skim the wood torso
of an upright bass, leaving the bow behind
for the kinesthetics of the body. We drop a new name
into the player and ruby into evening, feeling each
two-fingered pluck of Django Reinhardt's gypsy fingers
as they scamper about his guitar. You pull me close;
we slide into the engraved lines of old records
and find Paris in the rough *attouchement* of love.

Birdsongs

Having forgotten
what a line looks like
on a page, I unwrap
a notebook and tune
to Charlie Parker. *If I Should*
Lose You, wait for the record,
metal now and shiny,
to hiccup into
its grooves. Scattered
over an unseen stave of five
parallel lines, the blue
narcotic notes from
a saxophone scatter
like debris
in a wind tunnel.

Dénouement

The hours we keep are never reasonable.
Because we have forgotten to tap off
the hidden switch when we arrive,
the porch light stays on late,
yellows the stairwell with a broken moon.
Leaving the window cracked permits cold air
to wander through the hassled room,
reach our tired bodies and mimic
the scratch of a record played on a turntable.
It cracks and fractures in the bitter night.
Time drags like the lit end of a cigarette
while Roberta Flack spins
hours into things of gold.

In the end, we close the lid of the player
lay the jacket on the nightstand, sip
from a cup of tea and saunter toward sleep.
We tell time by the thermostat clocked
to a comfortable place, watch as the bulb
sings to the dark night and the crowded bed.

The Lost Valley

Bagpipes exist in multiple:

one plaid player breathes
with singular breaths
into the mouthpiece and sound

fills this world and the next.

A thousand players saturate
the amphitheater of Glencoe

one pipe
a million tones
reach out

for tiny warriors
setting out for sky.

Some Things Are Best Left

unfinished. Under terse brushstrokes,
draft marks appear on the rough canvas.
Graphite outlines whisper through
the beginning membranes of browns
surreptitious blues and yellow sugar marks.
But they don't harness camouflage
any better than flakes of black
which filter into view, translated
as two figures in the half green
landscape of the painting.

This is how you leave me,
half visible without the pink curve
of your lips on my skin. I can only
see your line fading to shadows
as you turn to leave. Without
the warmth of your hand inside the cuff
of my shirt, a blank space emerges.
Missing from our unfinished painting—
the final brushstroke, the kiss
that could coat the scarcity between us.

Look over and finish the scene:
fill in the borders. Maybe
you forgot to lick an envelope
or turn off the lamp before falling
asleep. Blend enough scarlet
to ease toward sunrise. Open
the shades when morning comes.

Allegorical Figure of the Schuylkill River

As if her skin was worthy to kill for, she appears
to be bathing herself, posing on a stub, perhaps
a tree cut to a stump, but who can tell?
It is after all, a painting, an allegory really—standing
for something else. To her right a woman knits
and in the background is *William Rush Carving His.*

It is the painter Eakins who took away her clothing,
aligned the lapis hair band to the mirror, lay the blue
chemise in a pile of clouds. Of course, softness
is a matter of taste, of perspective, of opinion.
What he offers is flesh on canvas, in certain light
frumpy as an uncut watermelon, in others
smooth as bark from a beech tree. Not given:
a pair of breasts, the moist triangle of hair,
the title of the book gripped on her right shoulder.
The shoulder itself, cast out of light, holds
the same mystery as the clothed statue.

There are words for clothing, words for being
without clothes, words for legs and buttocks.
But what words do we have to get into the mind
of the artist? However does a woman become
an allegory for a river? If not the Schuylkill,
then the Mississippi, the Nile, or the Amazon,
or a tiny unnamed river outside Seville.
There are times when a body is only a body,
but flesh, one could conjure, is always more than flesh.

Reading Anaïs Nin

The alphabet disappoints,
even with shapely curvatures,
sharp angles and mismatched
hieroglyphs. Letters wear masks,
syllables morph, and though
a sentence, with the generosity
of a fishing line, trails to the end
of a page then on and on, words
are no match for a torso bending
into another or a lick into the damp
velvet of sex. But the story
is what we have to ease us
into a lighted room. A painter
sketches his naked wife as she sleeps,
arranging her nightgown
so he can see her soft hair
and pink oak leaf lips
in the light she shies away from
when they make love.
In his studio he lays the sketches
around him on the floor until
he rises. When his wife enters,
he is bare, writhing
among his painted creations,
and in her envy she presses
onto him, hoping to surpass the art
he has set before her. But
in this brevity, they collapse
under the frailty of typed letters
on the page. If only they could
trace the rounded O or snuggle
into the caves of S, slip into
V and feel its depth, real and exact.

My Gargoyle Love

When we met, I studied your arms, your hands, your torso, the slant and heave of your breast as you breathed. Each time I took your crafted face in my hands, I began to sculpt you, polishing your beauty bright as a copper weathervane finding the half-light of four o-clock. To capture it, I ransomed my heart-labor for a gallery and fixtures from an exhibition on Main Street.

Every day, I mapped our partnership in iron with a thousand motions of a borrowed hammer. The first statue I fashioned according to your love—delicate, duplicating the softness of your hair as best I could. Soon our affection became damp; the droop of your eyelids found their way into my notebook.

We drifted, and I shaped a different profile: flattened eyebrows, dimpled nose, rough-edged teeth, dull and waxy hair. While the rain urged me on and sunshine disguised the motives of my regimen, the lust we once knew rusted so much that I forgot how your beautiful lips tenderly touched the crease of my forehead.

Arguments escalated to throwing wineglasses and your grandmother's brass candlesticks, to dents and forced inlays. Anything forged had to be broken. From right to left, I murdered your beauty with a chisel and sandpaper, with fire and knife. Love, gargoyled according to my wrath.

Then Eve Said Get a Grip, Man, It's Only An Apple

I try to slip into that memory
when we had no quarrels. Instead
I am looking at the fruit,
red as fire, round as stone
in my hand, an empty pit
at the place where I put my teeth.
Too quick, you said, *got to chew*
until the juices slide down.
Tastes like cottonseed, I tell you,
and see you are watching me
from the place where your legs meet.

Evie, my skin crawls as I snake
my way around, slip my tongue
hard into your mouth. Without effort
I taste the sap of your body, liking
that I own you. After a long time
I see that you are bleeding—
it hardly matters. I am not thinking
of our next walk or the smell
of lilacs in your hair. I hear you
laughing like a bird, and I am jealous
of how bright you look.

Reproductions

The visual representation of an object is different from the object itself.
—George Condo

After profiteroles, we debate
whether the haystacks framed
above the mock fireplace
are real or reproductions.

Without moving closer
it's impossible to tell
if they're painted or postered
or just so obvious

after art class and folded brochures
that the assumption, whichever
way it leans, is enough
to satisfy lazy viewers.

Are these the haystacks
that haunted Kandinsky
and summoned easels
en plein air?

Who cares? The amateur light
of pre-summer filters
with such surety through
a dappled lace curtain; silver forks

and hollowed spoons invite
reflection and refraction;
atoms race with torpedo speed
and sanction hypnosis—

the kind of sleep that horses
munching on seasonal hay
fall into, a forest-through-the-trees
tunnel vision

that answers questions of worth
with yeses and nos and articulated
definitions. No one believes
any more in the authenticity

of first sight, in the wonderment
that flat red bricks arranged
in steady configurations
mortared into ordinary mantle

can deliver to an open eye.
The challenge of recognition
is not as artless as eyes
would have us believe.

Hatshepsut's Bounty

When her fleet of five ships leaves
the red coast of Egypt for the Land of Punt,
the summer reeds bow dutifully,
but the gypsum-rich mud
floods the frothing banks with omens.

The sails, raised with twisted flax cortege,
balloon with the north wind. The vessel
drifts down the Red Sea to the Horn where
blackwood, juniper, and cinnamon bark
lurk in the forest awaiting wayward traders.
Once the resins of other sacred trees are packed
and secured in the hull, the bare chested
oarsmen scull the tepid waves north
again to the palace of Hatshepsut.

Despite the richly priced bounty, the desert
remains an unforgiving land, and the red disk
called Aten burns suspiciously, counting the days
to the end of the girl-king's sovereignty. With myrrh
smoldering in the morning light, she dons
a woven kilt, royal headdress and false beard,
watches with kohl-darkened eyes for Osiris.

As afternoon approaches, the pungent tang
of frankincense billows from an enameled clay pot,
the one that will shatter on the temple floor
when Thutmose turns her cartouches
and statues into rubble. While she waits,
gray *kyphi* smoke seeps into evening and
like a falcon, catches flight with the rising moon.

Bathed in palm wine, rinsed with the blue water
of the Nile, the pharaoh will be cut open
emptied, filled once more with salts and sawdust,
wrapped finally with the white regalia
of the dead. While her body,
sapped of liquid, sinks with kingly sloth
into the granite bones of the mortuary temple,

her name will be whittled away from obelisks
by crooked tools. To a petrified corpse,
the afterlife stinks like marsh dung
and the lonely sands sneak like thieves
through the cracks of history.

Parachutes

—for Agnés Humbert

She finds beauty in the explosion of bombs
pinwheeling above Krefeld's factory roofs

and in epilepsy's crescent dance fixed
to a spinner's emaciated and elegant frame;

in the short relief given to eyes burning
from thread dust winged and airborne,

from spools of rayon wound with typist fingers
scarred by fabricated silk, its acid and viscose

falling like miniature parachutes
in mechanized, pus filled jumps.

It is August, 1942 and words like
revenge, reprisal, resistance

translate slowly without soap, in watery
porridge, and in stolen strips of fabric

bandaging clandestine feet. Some
of the prisoners wear clogs. Some of them

swallow the acid. Some die, some do not.
Before a delousing shower, she bundles

a pile of clothes, clutches them
like an unopened parachute. Hers is not

the parcel of long blond hair shaved off
and thrown into the furnace that heats

the steam room. Even the prostitutes
gaggle with outrage as guards gawk

without paying for glimpses of what some
might call nakedness. Sometimes she finds

reconciliation in selecting between
devastation, defeat and whatever stands

as the opposite: when the guard plunges
only hands into run-off acid vats. Only hands.

In the company of air raids overhead,
locked in the infirm walls of a cellar

she finds that the one comfort for acid girls
who make parachutes out of enemy silk

is to pee on their shirts, wrap them
defiantly like chrysalis silk around

burned and blistered hands and imagine
the sky filling with open, paper-white poppies.

Toward a New Deal

—FDR Memorial, Washington D.C

Then, when bread lines lengthened
over patched city streets, when
shovels dug and wrenches could hardly
strengthen the dignity of a man,
we needed the fireside voice, needed
photographs framing a whole torso,
a wool cloak covering what we could not
see. Concrete to be mixed, dams
to be erected, forests to be seeded.
Buttons to be sewn, war to be waged.
The weight of it all held up by arms
sturdy as the spokes of any wheel.

In bronze, another view receives us:
molded in clay, reborn in the furnace.
Molten cast, sprues severed, metal pounded,
patina'd, and polished. The man
who stood in leg braces and promised
to help us feed ourselves, to build ourselves
up, to stand again on our own,
rests now in the wheelchair
once hidden by lap blankets and desktops,
by reluctance and toughness
and charity's need to shield those
already broken from more brokenness.

Hands to be traced on colored paper,
tables to be set with candles, storefronts
to be opened and potholes filled,
wounds to be sutured with more

than words, we wheel together
without crutches toward a new deal
now that we know how.

Katharine of Fenwick

Grey hair upswept
with pins and lack of purpose,
turtleneck, denim shirt
movie star profiles lost under
skin turned by woodcutter's tools,
the fiery brunette with thin waist
and angled New England nose
braved these foggy shores
into her ninth decade with the elegance
of a egret stepping through silt and
slow moving waters. She invited
Spencer Tracy only once.

Away from the click-click-click
of cellophane trailing the tin emptiness
of a finished reel, away
from the unfiltered white of a bulb burning
onto the letterbox of a dappled screen,
somewhere in the marshes outside
Old Saybrook, Kate rowed the boat
of anonymity and found home
where red-winged blackbirds
echo in the tall reeds and herons
turn to silver in the crisp gloam of evening.

Manana Island

There is never enough to say
about goats, Manana goats, the ones who
roam freely, unfenced, around the island

and eat cranberries and juniper greens
and stay out past sunset, if they like.
There is never enough to say

about cormorants building future nests—
for it is summer, and yearlings
roam freely, unfenced around the island

and nest no more, at least not now.
With sun two hours past its zenith,
there is never enough to say

about sky and water comingling, merging
like co-conspirators with the conduit of air
roaming freely, unfenced, around the island.

Butterflies come and go, like goats,
as they please, like wheat grass or poets
who never have enough to say
roaming freely, unfenced, around the island.

Hall of African Mammals

Gemsbok, sable, kudu,
bongos, and elands
their varied horns of silken hair
wound like tornadoes
curved and coiled
sharp and weapony
gallant and useful
sly and slight.
Their bodies, even
in diorama poses
move with the effortlessness
of whispers. I feel guilty
for exposing their stealth.

For a moment, I understand
the desire to harvest these horns
and display their trophy beauty.
The woman with the camera wants this too.
To be momentarily as beautiful
as the scimitar-horned oryx of the plains
would be victory for anyone
who ever thought herself
ugly. And it is, after all,
our ugliness we're trying to escape
when we kill.

Standing here
before the hornless okapi
I can be only jealous
of his fake permanence,
of the perfectly preserved
loveliness captured
in pose.

First Person

As the first person my first
instinct is to be a tyrant,
asking small animals to move.
I am fearless, yet frightened,
and I am jinxed. I have the ability
to stand against germs. The first
person is me. I believe in myself.

The third person is one or they,
he or she, Wendy or Alexander.
The elephant dances with the chairman.
Billy is left handed but plays right field.
Two blocks from the place her car
would be towed, they sat together
in that coffee shop, watching women
walk poodles down October streets.

Second person is a life of your own,
particularly strange and secondary,
possessing thy name, rare
but commanding. Perhaps thou
art the dream voice, a little delicate,
not quite understandable,
like a memory recalled then lost
in a dark hallway somewhere
where you are not.

Today, I am the first person, thinking
of your last remembered life,
one when they were peasants
in Ancient Greece, speaking to gods
and dreaming of our future.

Prototype

Bless the first day of class
in its confined clutter. Notebooks
stacked and piled like sculptures
that say to the first lesson, *I am ready*
for you to feed me. Catapult us
into the realms of academia.
Picture chimpanzees swallowing
pineapple-white sheets in open cages.

Get your hands dirty, I tell them,
love the pages, the print, smell it
and remember papyrus. Break
the spine, hold it up to the light:
tell me who you are, author, tell
me your secrets; help me make sense
of your world. Transmogrify.
Cave dwellers, hierophants—make friends
with the exclamation point, bond
with the asterisk. Play with dirt.
Play with dirty words.

How to Visit Your Alma Mater

It should be quiet when you visit:
choose study days or weekends when students
filter out of dormitory shells in soundless trickles,
ensuring an eerie solitude you'll recognize
as the lonely thump of acorns outside
the dorm room when your parents drove away.

It must be autumn: pine needles crinkle
under feet walking from the parking lot
to campus as the movie of your life
flashes back, each image framed
in an old October light. Red-haired
girls saunter down the same sidewalks
where new buildings startle you.
Think of them as the growth and maturation
you were promised during those first days,
when another autumn felt crisp
as the unbroken binding of a textbook.

Take the boyfriend you dreamed of and show him
the nooks you crannied into: your first classroom
where the discovery of Sappho and Rilke
saved your life not once, but again
and again each time winter clouds
recycled their white pages into spring rain,
and you scurried under words for shelter.

When the man you plan to marry
enters you in a library study room,
the nuances and doom of pixie girlhood

disappear as new myths are created,
ones where dreaming no longer aches
but permeates like red maple sunshine
on your wise and blissful face.

"There Was an Occupation"

Alice B. Toklas is falling apart,
Gertrude Stein is tinkering with bread knives
and apple seeds have nowhere to fall

before a jar of picnic songs, the ripe kind—
sung without anemia or rancid pudding.
Alice B. Toklas is falling apart.

Her hair—wiry as Shakespeare's fluorescent quill
and coned like bullet tracks across dull brick walls
where apple seeds have nowhere to fall

in the winter of 1941—has turned grey twigs,
silica, and Spanish moss. Fourteen cents. Bickering.
Alice B. Toklas has fallen apart,

and Gertrude refuses the barley. Relinquishes rooms
and candlesticks. Blue pitted shifts and suggestions spinning,
meaning the apple seeds are nowhere, fallow,

nor tabletops and pocket watches never mind handshakes.
Before and render and abandon. Before and bombs,
before Alice B. Toklas began to fall apart,
before the apples and their seeds began to fail.

Mrs. Dalloway

There are, of course, flowers;
they fill her hands before any vase,
but even in their glass tomb, she sees
the void they have lent their lives to.
Once the guests arrive, she sinks
between the desire for the most
satisfying success and the deep
and heeding certainty that none of it
prevents the day's observable artifacts
from passing through the clear,
choking air of an open window.

Inkwell

carry blame
like a camel's hump
through the vacant lot of now
past this roll-top desk

stop worrying
about humming
periwinkles or the rumble
of closing elevator doors

that never find their way
into a line; stop trying
to catch words
that blow away
through apprehension's window

tackle this maiden world
with discipline

give fingers
to the hurricane

Transcontinental Migrations

Sparrows flit in midday sun
outside my window, and a titmouse
with burnt tuft and dusty blue plumes
hurries into the verdant hands
of the cedar hedge that reaches past
the second floor. Here I am

pecking away at black, lettered cubes
constructing a different bird, the one
who tiptoes out of notebook sketches
and photographs sequestered
in the trustworthy memory of the hard drive.

I've been trying to recreate
this west coast sand piper scurrying
across the slate mirror of sand, the precise
trail of prints eluding the fast cover
of wooly surf, the coordinated
gracefulness of this sea bird pursuing
a feast of insects and small crustaceans.

Channel Islands wear the hazy disguise
of a veiled sun concealing the sprawl of land
just off the California coast where my piper
studies the etymology of sand and chooses
an invisible pockmark for food. I love

the repetition of her persistence.
I love that she is one of many, each
as immediate in its search as every other
winged creature on any coast or forest,
in any meadow or painted green lawn.

It's this immediacy that I cannot recreate
despite hours of cross-outs and deleted
versions deposited and sucked away.
The migrations of pen across paper
take me from the ambulant aubade
of the Oxnard surf to an open window
on a humid east coast afternoon.

My ear follows the arc of persistent chirps
that layer in piping waves, perpetual
through untall conifers that may not be
as steadfast as oceans nor as far away
and inviting as a beach. But this day's bird,

a henna feathered cardinal, peppers around
the loose landscape of home with its own
perfectly evolved beak. He manifests
not as an opposite, but as one of many
pursuing a good meal, a kindhearted mate,
and the chance to align with the hidden magnet
of the earth's sunlit axis.

Byron and Shelley

As we trudged along the varied paths
of the Highland Way you did not let go
to cry, though legs ached with pain
and skewed nerves slipped out of place
screaming for you to stop.

Our last night before we go home,
I read Trelawny's *Recollections*
of the Last Days of Shelley and Byron:
Percy's funeral muddies my mind,
but I cannot unhinge the sable-eyed rival
or the torture of a lame and disfigured foot
that shamed Byron all his days. How skilled
we are at pushing our deformities into
the deepest alcove then turning away from them,
lest they outpace and overcome us.

A red-haired boy—more than a boy—
a young man—travels with us
on the flight back home. His father
who is grey and wears glasses
accompanies him. I see that the boy
is blind, and think he is—how
to say this kindly—lame of mind,
though as I watch him and his father
pace back to their seats, I see that he is
purely sightless, and I feel cruel for thinking
it was something more. All this time

I thought that it was me we were walking for,
the mess upon me and the volume of days

yet unwritten tensing with uncertainty,
smudged with hieroglyphs of caned figures
and the imposing arc of wheels.

Waiting out the rain in Philadelphia
my head slumped in exhaustion, your legs
extended in a futile stretch, I grasp
what it was we were really walking for:

the German girls whom we'll not see again;
for Gerry, our sturdy guardian, agile as a buoy,
flecks of white in his hair and a harness of years
on his back; for the moments between the rain;

what every boy's blindness wants to possess;
for Byron's feet and the contents of Shelley's coat pockets
washed up on a shore we haven't yet visited
and may not ever walk upon.

Giverny

One can meditate for days
on a painting, but minute to minute
all is chaos among bamboo, willows,
and the fanned leaves of gingkoes.

Until I reach Monet's boat studio,
even the lilies with their compass points,
pink and white, cannot orient me
toward the man with a beard and hat
and brush. I've lost the painting
in the deflection of my own eyes.

Legions of irises, some small and delicate,
open like butterflies with soft
corrugated petals. Others stand grand
and proud, with petals like dragon tongues
white, yellow, purple, and a kind of midnight
that makes me believe in the failure
of any reproduction. Peonies explode
like pom-poms; pansies with painted faces
tilt their heads as if spying on me,
the only reluctant one among the bunches.

The paper cups of poppies hold the fate
of fat bees and a few white moths
and signal red exactly the way Monet did,
deliberately, dancing, dipping again
and again for more light—creating it
with a different shade of yellow,
a smaller brush, tomorrow's noon hour.

Do the immediate gardens of Giverny
overshadow a partial canvas?
Once bullfrogs, brazen and enduring,
began to croak in conversation,
the tourists blurred into a mutable
conglomerate of lupines and forget-me-nots,
and skies which had mulled in clouds
all morning reclaimed the mirror
of the pond: then I could see.

The Resuscitating Tonic of Make-Believe

After the fifth or sixth closing of a now tethered
hard back edition, (her grandmother's copy)
she sent *Anne of Green Gables* back
to the bookcase without ceremony or accolades
with only the guarded impulses of a pact
made between bosom friends: a girl and a book.

Even before her young lips knew
the timid inklings of what might
be later recognized as true love,
she had the entire exploit pinned down
like tissue paper patterned onto checkered gingham.

Someday, she'd bring him, her own Gilbert,
whoever he might manifest as, wherever
she might find him, to red clay sea cliffs of Anne's
Prince Edward Island, leave the silk dress,
tuxedo jacket and champagne toasts behind
at the chapel, board the ferry and seek out
the lake of the shining waters, where fields
of tall grasses swoon in the breeze and hollyhocks
chime like wedding bells. But someday seems

an unreachable planet when one is thirteen.
The resuscitating tonic of make-believe begins
to peter out like a late August waterfall; thirsty
pragmatism piles up where once fluid imaginings
squeezed between a book's secretive folds. Flipping
to the last page, she predicts that happily-ever-after
will look good pressed into malleable paper,
but such endings, with their achieved resolutions,
belong only to red-headed heroines, not real girls
who collect bookmarks and play tuba in the band.

Reconnaissance

The chairs they sit in are yellow,
freshly painted, at least it seems so to me
sitting by myself, trying to be invisible.
I bury my head in a book and spy

on the balding father with his daughter
buying pizza at the country store. Her hair
is the color of straw. She wears too much make up
but is content to play cards with her dad
on the store's front porch. Sometimes
I imagine what they're thinking,

but I always feel conspicuous
even when I find myself alone.
Half of me acts as a voyeur, observing
the man who mows the lawn in rows
that slant just off the parallel, removes
his hat and wipes his brow with an old
yellow handkerchief. His daughter is
leaving for college and he feels mulched
and wishes the sky would rain a bit.

The other half of me wishes herself the target
of the spy. I imagine the old woman
swimming the short diameter of the lake
will go home and write a poem about me,
the young girl in the yellow sweater who
surfaces on the far side of cove, sitting
on a rock too small to see.

Or that the fisherman hides his canvas
in the keel of his boat and switches oars
for thin brushes whenever he feels like drifting
inconspicuously through a field of water lilies
or a gathering of ducks. Whenever the rhythm
of rowing slants just off the parallel,
he uses his invisibility and paints.

And just when white seems too obvious,
and world's inhabitants seem too ordinary
and predictable, he spies a hint of yellow,
maybe a sweater, maybe a silk chemise
with small, elegant buttons, maybe a scarf
worn around shoulders, or was that her hair?
This tells him exactly how much yolk
to blend in, and how to dot the lily's center
and capture variable light on a sunless day.

Either way, I play the coy, indistinct watcher
finding stealth in the bold oaks and
greening poplars, choosing the unassuming
bisque scarf and gawking with greedy eyes
over the edges of *Great Expectations*,
the old edition, the one with yellow edges.

After Inspecting Brassaï's *Graffiti*

At Musée d'Art Moderne
I notice the construct of silhouetted
stick figures juxtaposed above a door;
one's triangular body tells me
to go into a different *salle*. There,
I find another version of graffiti
on the door in front of me as I sit down.
This is not art someone has written.
My bladder agrees, but against this angst
and all treachery of the world's turmoil
another has revolted: *Yes it is—*
Art is what you make of it. Such words
delight me at first; they affect such openness,
pretend pluralism, and compel acceptance
of every sapling of discontent that arises
at seeing paint spread like entrails on the floor.
What you make of it . . . as if anyone could
wake and slither into anarchy and come out
with the paraphrase of a quail egg. I go out
and back to the exhibits, back to the violence
and spectacle of color and form. Seeking out
other dimensions, I walk into a room wrapped
in giant spools of gray, industrial felt.
At the end of one hall, a sculpture in straw
creates the illusion of an airplane; a thousand
pairs of scissors spear its shape. *Art is*
what you make of it? I need to go back:
digging into my bag and finding a pen
I scratch the last two words into blackness.

About the Author

This is Amy Nawrocki's second collection with Homebound Publications. Her previous book, *Four Blue Eggs*, was the Poetry Prize finalist for 2013. Her three chapbooks were published by Finishing Line Press. With her husband, Eric D. Lehman, she has written three Connecticut history books, most recently *Literary Connecticut*. She teaches English and Creative Writing at the University of Bridgeport and lives in Hamden, Connecticut.

HOMEBOUND
PUBLICATIONS

At Homebound Publications we publish books written by soul-oriented individuals putting forth their works in an effort to restore depth, highlight truth, and improve the quality of living for their readers.

As an independent publisher we strive to ensure that "the mainstream is not the only stream." With the release of each book, we aim to introduce new perspectives that will directly aid mankind in the trials we face at present as a global village.

So often in this age of commerce, entertainment supersedes growth; books of lesser integrity but higher marketability are chosen over those with much-needed truth but a smaller audience. We focus on the quality of the truth and insight present before any other considerations.

At Homebound Publications we value authenticity and fresh ideas. From the submissions process where we choose our projects right down to the crafting of each finished book, our intention is to provide a moment of solace and insight for our readers.

CPSIA information can be obtained
at www.ICGtesting.com
Printed in the USA
FFOW04n2146170315
11907FF

9 781938 846694